YOUR KNOWLEDGE HAS VALUE

Imprint:

Copyright © 2010 GRIN Verlag, Open Publishing GmbH
Print and binding: Books on Demand GmbH, Norderstedt Germany
ISBN: 978-3-668-18410-7

This book at GRIN:

http://www.grin.com/en/e-book/319004/how-jazz-music-supported-black-pride-social-change-and-political-activity

Anonym

How Jazz Music Supported Black Pride, Social Change and Political Activity

GRIN Publishing

GRIN - Your knowledge has value

Since its foundation in 1998, GRIN has specialized in publishing academic texts by students, college teachers and other academics as e-book and printed book. The website www.grin.com is an ideal platform for presenting term papers, final papers, scientific essays, dissertations and specialist books.

Visit us on the internet:

http://www.grin.com/

http://www.facebook.com/grincom

http://www.twitter.com/grin_com

Goethe- Universität Frankfurt am Main

How jazz music supported Black pride, social change and political activity

Jazz music in American culture

WS 10/11

HF: Amerikanistik
HF: Historische Ethnologie
Ps: Jazz music in American culture

Contents

1. Introduction

It is important to make people aware of the largely untold story of the key role jazz music had in helping to shape Black pride and encouraging social change as well as political activity in the United States. For this reason, I choose to write about this subject in my paper. In my opinion ways of non- violence that supports the process of change in a society should be given particular attention. I want to emphasis that this work should be taken as a theoretical attempt for it cannot be proved to which extent jazz music had an influence on social change and how things would have developed without the upcoming of jazz music.

My sources for this paper were mainly online sources. To this very specific subject the internet offered more information. So the basic question which will be discussed in this paper is how culture has a meaning on Black Revolution.

2. Jazz and its roots in slave music

When we go back and think of slaves working on plantations it becomes clear that the only way they could express themselves was through art and more specific music. It was the only form of expression which wasn't instantly repressed as it happened to political and economic opinions. Afro-American/ American Negro work songs were the direct forerunner of blues music (Jones, 15).

So it can be seen as a tradition of African American music to broach the issue of social, economic and political struggle. For jazz has its roots in early blues music, this tradition had been picked up. This tradition has been continuing until today in Gospel, Soul, Blues, Reggae and Rap music. The struggle must not necessarily be expressed by the lyrics but can also be expressed through the music itself. Just think of Coltrane's saxophone playing in "Alabama" for example. The song is throughout melancholic.

3. The situation of early African American jazz musicians

Early jazz music such as Billie Holliday's or John Coltrane's can only be understood by viewing the connection to the Civil Rights Movement from 1955 to 1968 and by considering the conditions of Black people at the times of Jim Crow.

In the 1920s, the USA had to face a greater extent of segregation than to any point of time after the Civil War had ended. Southern African Americans had been denied to vote, several rights of appeal and the possibility to move to certain areas were refused. Furthermore, they could not register for numerous schools, were not treated in many hospitals and miscellaneous institutions. African Americans even were excluded from churches, businesses and farms. No abandonment of Jim Crow laws was conceivable, not even a trend of loosening the discriminating code was in sight. Peretti claims that during the 1920s Jim Crow laws were even intensified. An additional threat for African Americans was the Ku Klu Klan and other white radical groups. After jazz was established in the north, it began to make its way up to the south of the Ohio River and the Mason Dixie Line. The descendants of slaves were faced with people who insulted, harmed them physically and even took their lives. These inhuman actions mostly happened in public and were displayed so everyone could watch the humiliations. (Peretti 177).

Although slavery was abolished in the USA in 1865, by the end of the Civil Rights Movement Blacks were still not treated equally to Whites. For a long period Black and White jazz musicians were not allowed to perform together in public. In the early 1930s, Black and White jazz musicians could not play any concerts together and could not perform together in clubs. The Jim Crow laws of the Southern states were acceptilated between 1876 and 1965. Although "Separate but equal" was the legal doctrine Blacks were disadvantaged in every respect (www.thethankfulheritage.org).

This was also the case in Montgomery, Alabama. On public buses Blacks could only occupy the rear seats while White people were privileged to sit down. Rosa Parks, a woman of African American origin in 1955 refused to give up her seat for a White person. As a result she was arrested and brought to justice. The National Association for the Advancement of Colored People (NAACP) complained in court and won. On 13 November 1956, the Supreme Court confirmed that racial segregation was unconstitutional and repealed the segregation on buses (www.blackhistory.com).

While and after giving a concert African American jazz musicians were confronted with violence as well. Often they played for a White audience but had to keep away from them anyway after the show. If musicians were for instance talked to by White women, they risked being accused by way of example for molesting.

In many cases African Americans at jazz event could get involved with the police very easily. Sometimes when people would lean on the rope that was put in front of the stage, to wish for a song, which should be played by the band, the police threaded them as they had commited a violation. In a lot of cases even women were beaten down. White sometimes even would feel provoked when a Black[1] man in jazz club would take a drink from a White woman. (Peretti 179).

Maybe this is why especially Black jazz musicians, that were also descendants of slaves, developed a certain sense for racial discrimination and inequality.

4. How and why jazz musicians took action with their music
4.1. John Coltrane- Revolution of the psyche
Incidents like the bus boycott or sit-ins occurred during the Civil Rights Movement which was a worldwide political movement for equality before the law, between about 1950 and 1980. There were many organizations like NUL, NALC, SCEF, FOR, NCLC, *NAACP, SNCC, CORE*, SCLC and SDS that fought for the political and economic independency of African Americans in the USA. The Civil Rights Movement and the Black Power Movements shaped moral pressure on musicians and influenced them to take action as well. There were numerous jazz musicians who used their music to revolt and express their anger about the oppression they experienced (Reader: Jazz music in American culture).

For example how John Coltrane did in his song *Alabama*. Coltrane wrote the song *Alabama* in response to the bombing of a Baptist Church where four Black girls were killed. It was a racist attack by some Ku Klux Klan members. It is even said that Coltrane patterned his saxophone playing on Martin Luther King's funeral speech he held for the four girls who were killed. Coltrane's grandfather introduced him to politics

---

[1] Although Peretti spelled "black" with a small "b", in this paper "Black" is spelled with a capital "B" to underline that the spelling with a small "b" refers to a color and the spelling with a capital "B" refers to a social group.

and gave him several books by Black people that he should read. His grandfather who was a reverend influenced Coltrane a lot and raised his interest for politics (Kahn 34).

If you listen to Coltrane, in some parts you can hear the rage he tried to express. The drummer as well rises from a whisper to a pounding rage when he plays the song *Alabama*. The whole mood of the song is very melancholic but still hopeful. This shows not only the anger of the oppression and the events but the sadness as well. Coltrane's sound was definitively shaped consciously but also subconsciously by the developing Civil Rights Movement that extended in the US in the late 1950's and 1960's.

He did not agree with W.E.B. Du Bois's concept of a "double-consciousness". For one being and American but also being reminded of being a "negroe" by other people's reaction. Having a double-consciousness could mean being able to have two perspectives but implies certain ambivalence as well (Reader: Einführung in die amerikanische Kultur und Kulturwissenschaft 87).

For Coltrane there was nothing in between. Just like for Malcolm X, a politician and a radical leader of the Civil Rights Movement Coltrane rather took a firm stand concerning the situation of Black people. It was expressed in the way he played his music. In his opinion there was no need any longer for Black culture waiting for the appreciation by White society but there was definitely a need that Black people started to appreciate their own culture themselves. Coltrane and Malcolm presented an image of a decolonized Black selfhood (Saul 260-261).

Coltrane's famous album "A Love Supreme" and Malcolm X's biography gained so much attention for they represented counterimages of the working-class African American. They did not accept the image of the African American as inferior. In the case of Coltrane denying this role, meant denying bebob's irony and presenting a religious, self-discovering, very personal music (Saul 263-264).

In Coltrane's opinion, playing in an authentic way, meant living authentically. He in 1958 said that most musicians were interested in the truth, they had to be, for saying something in a musical way was expressing the truth (Kahn 36).

Coltrane and Malcolm convicted those who tried to conform to a mainstream White America. Concerning these accusations, the two images defined by Malcolm became popular: The "house negroe" attempting to please his master and the "field negroe" revolting against his master. Martin Luther King, who promoted the image of one day Blacks and Whites being united was also condemned by Malcolm of being a "house negroe" (Saul 263-264).

In spite and sometimes by reason of their talents, jazz musicians couldn't get away from the racism's humiliation. Coltrane's himself had experienced a lot of racist violations. His best friend was beaten to death by the police. The famous free jazz drummer Sonny Murray actually lost his finger from a racist attack (www.socialistreview.org.uk).

4.2. Billie Holiday- A "Strange Fruit"

Billie Holiday was one of the most influential Afro American jazz singers since the beginning of Jazz music. She grew up in a poor family and always dreamed of being a singer.

Early she was confronted with racial inequality. Her father had died in a hospital's "negroe hall" (a separated space for African Americans, with poor conditions), which she could never forget (Clarke 203).

Being a young African American woman, living in times of lynching, Billie experienced a lot of racism. Her probably most famous song *Strange Fruit* draws attention to the shocking conditions of African Americans in the 1930s. Many people were touched emotionally by the way she presented the song (Clarke 1-25).

When Billie first performed the song, she got so emotional and sang it so intensely that tears started running down her cheeks (Clarke 200).

It appeared as if she had written it herself, although at first when the song was presented to her by Abel Meeropol, a Jewish high-school teacher from the Bronx, she did not even understand what it was about. Later she could even identify with the song and express the pain of Black people who lived in a country where they feared to be lynched (Clarke 1-25).

The lyrics of *Strange Fruit* which came out in 1956 are:

"Southern trees bear a strange fruit,
Blood on the leaves and blood at the root,
Black bodies swinging in the southern breeze,

strange fruit hanging from the poplar trees.

Pastoral scene of the gallant south,
the bulging eyes and the twisted mouth,
Scent of magnolias, sweet and fresh,
then the sudden smell of burning flesh.

Here is fruit for the crows to pluck,
for the rain to gather, for the wind to suck,
for the sun to rot, for the trees to drop,
here is a strange and bitter crop"

(www.songtexte.com).

The poem, about the lynching of Black human beings originally was written by Abel Meeropol.[2]

The song refers to the lynching in the south. There is blood on the leaves from the dead bodies. To that time the south was always viewed as idyllic: this is what "pastoral scenes" wants to express. The lyrics show the brutality and cruelty in an idyllic setting and the image of a fruit is used representatively for the human body hanging from a tree.

Everyone knew about the lynching, even the government in Washington. Not even the government tried to stop the lynching. The NAACP for years attempted to abolish lynching by an anti-lynching law which had not been accepted (Clarke 203).

Billie may not have been a political activist or a great talker but through her singing she had the ability to give people an understanding of the suffering African Americans experienced throughout history. The way she used her voice in her singing made it sound like a painful crying. It helped to assume the pain of African Americans in times of lynching.

Shortly after she had performed *Strange Fruit* for the very first time, a picture of her appeared in *Times Magazine*. In fact, Billie Holiday was the first Black women whose picture was printed in *Times Magazine*. After they had printed her picture, others followed (Clarke 200).

---

[2] He did not use his real name to publish the poem. His pen name is Lewis Allan.

This shows how influential jazz musicians could be and how they influenced change.

4.3. Louis Armstrong- the "Uncle Tomming" entertainer?

Louis Armstrong was an African American trumpeter. He had the reputation of the "Uncle Tomming" entertainer (Gebhardt 84).

He was an autodidact and became a band leader and singer, actor and writer. He influenced jazz more than anyone else before. He is known for his very special innovative style. Armstrong was backbitten by black activists and black musicians for playing in a stereotypical way because he performed for mostly white listeners he handled racial issues in a very non-obvious way. His song „Black and Blue", which was involved in a famous musical, was recorded in 1929. If you heard the song's words outside of the show, sung by a black man, at that time, it was a heavy and precarious utterance. Armstrong transmitted U.S. culture during the time of the cold war by playing jazz across the board. There came up more riots in connection to desegregation of public schools. Armstrong spoke his mind concerning this and scathed his country. In 1957, the National Guard prohibited nine black students to go inside a high school. This incident is also known as the Little Rock Crisis. Thereupon Armstrong refused to play a tour in the Soviet Union declaring the way his people in the South were treated, the government „could go to hell" (http://musiced.about.com).

At the very first glance the image of the "Uncle Tomming" entertainer might have been fitting but through his action he proved that he possessed more political consciousness and pride than it seemed.

4.4. Charlie Parker- From swing to bebop

There were jazz musicians who separated themselves from their instruments and saw them very consciously as an artifact. Charlie "Bird" Parker, the famous jazz musician, on his saxophone rather tried to sound like the human voice when it cried (Jones, 30).

Parker was one of the first to play bebob. This new group of bebobers no longer played earlier forms of jazz as White swing and Dixieland music; they didn't play bebob in a pop musical manner either. Instead they tried to play a more conscious style of jazz. As

Gebhardt mentions, Jones sees two motivations for this transformation. For one the attempt to interpret blues in their own way, their unwillingness to adapt to already existing jazz styles and American mainstream. It can be assumed that there was an influence in African American's thinking by the different genres of the music they played or heard. Including Parker's sway in phrasing and accent a black consciousness in jazz music came up. Musicians as Gillespie, Parker and Monk did no longer care if people would listen to their music, which was a crucial turning point in relation to formal American culture (Gebhardt 80-84).

Charlie Parker, just like John Coltrane as African Americans denied playing swing which was mainly played by Whites; this can be interpreted as a form of resistance and a form of liberation as well.

5. Music as an instrument of protest

5.1. The upcoming of bebob
With their amazing new techniques, all known rhythmic conventions were disdained. Former song structures were partly kept and new fancy melodies were included. Critics named the new upcoming music "bebob". This kind of music asked for listeners fully attention and did not stay in the background discreet. Bebob emphasized the tendency of jazz being played in nightclubs. This accompanied the loss of jazz's reputation being a lucrative and accepted kind of music in American society. This drew attention to numerous musicians who strived for individuality as well (Kahn 37).

5.2. We shall overcome
There were certain songs that played an enormous role during the Civil Rights Movement: For example *We Shall Overcome* which original's title was „I Shall Overcome". This song is rooted very deep in the African American culture. It was so popular during the Civil Rights Movement because it motivated the people to stand up for their rights and stand together. It was sung as a protest song, first in 1945, when striking tobacco workers in Charleston, S.C. sang it on their picket line. By the 1950s, the song was adapted by the young followers of the African American Civil Rights Movement. This is how it very promptly became the movement's unofficial anthem.

The lines of *We Shall Overcome* were sung on protest marches, in sit-ins in colleges and while being beaten up by the police during riots. It made the activists minds strong and let them forget the pain of their bodily injuries while sitting in a jail cell questioning if they would still be alive the next day. When the long years of struggle finally ended and President Lyndon Johnson promised to fight so all Americans could vote he included a last promise: "We shall overcome." The lyrics are (www.loc.gov):

" We shall overcome, some day.
Oh, deep in my heart, I do believe, we shall overcome, some day.
We'll walk hand in hand, some day.
Oh, deep in my heart, we shall live in peace, some day.
Oh, deep in my heart, we shall all be free, some day.
Oh, deep in my heart, we are not afraid today.
Oh, deep in my heart, we shall overcome, some day.
Oh, deep in my heart, I do believe. We shall overcome, some day. "[3]
(www.lyrics.de).

The jazz community was somehow leading the Civil Rights Movement. Several jazz musicians played benefit concerts to support the Civil Rights Movement. So it is evident that jazz music and the Civil Rights Movement went hand in hand. „CORE" has been one of the most powerful organizations to navigate the Civil Rights Movement from the late 1940s' until today. They act by Gandhi's principle of nonviolent civil disobedience. „CORE" took action by organizing sit-ins in the 1950s and 1960s. They had freedom rides to fight segregationist methods in the United States as well (www.artsjournal.com).

Jazz music at the time of the Civil Rights Movement was used to make a statement. It can be compared to blues music from which it actually originates, which was used on the plantation to strengthen the cohesion among the slaves. The same phenomenon can be observed with hip hop music that has its roots in jazz and blues music. It is used to make a statement and to denounce social injustice, as well. How music can have an

---

[3] "We Shall Overcome" was a typical, early protest song and played a major role in the Civil Rights Movement. Originally it was written by pastor Charles Albert Tindley in 1903. He sang it as a gospel song.

impact on society is proofed by reggae music that traditionally criticizes the system and the leftovers of slavery- mental slavery.

6. Conclusion

It is hard to say, what would have been without the rise of jazz music. No one knows for sure if the Civil Rights Movement would have developed the way it did, without the mental and political support of early African American jazz musicians. I think in this showed that music can have direct attention to certain subjects and situations. Music is in the position to transmit feelings to a populace. Several jazz musicians and icons functioned as emancipated examples. Their influence and the influence of their music and actions could have motivated people to take political action, to emancipate themselves from mental slavery and stand up for their dignity and their pride. Art can be a very powerful medium. As it is mentioned in this paper jazz music could bring Black and White performers together. This was a first step to a crucial change in society, politics and people's mind.

7. Sources

7.1. Works cited

1. Buschendorf, Christa. Reader WS 08/09 : Einführung in die amerikanische Kultur und Kulturwissenschaft 87.

2. Clarke, Donald. Billie Holiday- Wishing on the Moon. Trans. Barbara schaden und Ingeborg Schober. München: Piper, 1995.

3. Gebhardt, Nicholas. Going for Jazz. Chicago: The University Press of Chicago, 2001.

4. Jones, LeRoi. Blues People- Negroe Music in White America. New York: William Morrow and Company, 1967.

5. Kahn, Ashley. A Love Supreme. Berlin: Rogner & Bernhard GmbH & Co. Verlag, 2004.

6. Peretti, Burton W. The Creation of Jazz. Illinois: University of Illinois Press, 1992.

7. Saul, Scott. Freedom is, Freedom ain't. Cambridge, Massachusetts: Harvard University Press, 2003.

8. Völz, Johannes: Reader WS 10/11. Seminar- Jazz music in American culture.

7.2. Internetsources:

1. www.artsjournal.com/jazzbeyondjazz/2009/01/civil_rights-jazz_document_196.html. Date of access: 10.02.11.

2. www.blackhistory.com/cgi-bin/blog.cgi?cid=52&reading=1&blog_id=60675. Date of access: 06.02.11.

3. www.lyrics.de/songtext/deanreed/weshallovercome_65922.html. Date of access: 15.02.11.

4. www.loc.gov/teachers/lyrical/songs/overcome.html. Date of access: 16.02.11.

5. http://musiced.about.com/od/blackhistorymonth/p/larmstrong.htm. Date of access: 20.02.11.

6. www.socialistreview.org.uk/article.php?articlenumber=8606. Date of access: 11.02.11.

7. www.songtexte.com/songtext/billie-holiday/strange-fruit-73d70a55.html. Date of access: 07.02.11.

8. www.thethankfulheritage.org/tour.html. Date of access: 03.02.11.